Aging With Ungirdled Passion

By Tracy Kunzler

Follow Tracy Kunzler and Ungirdled Passion:
www.facebook.com/UngirdledPassion
Twitter: @Ungirdled

Dedication

To my amazing husband who supports me in so many ways; our sons who I am proud to call mine (and I hope never write a book about me); and my cherished girlfriends living with ungirdled passion who delight, inspire and strengthen me. Thanks for all your stories, the laughs and the shoulders. A very special thanks goes to artistic geniuses and good friends Vicki Bruner for the cover illustration and Lucy Alfriend Thacker for the cover design.

Table of Contents

Bling For Your Private Thing

The Right Mix Of Thongs and Granny Panties
In Our Friendship Drawers

Shift Happens. It's Best To Be A Man About It.

Body Parts Aren't The Only
Things That Wander With Age

My Perfect Sleep Number Is Chardonnay

Sex Drive In Park; Needs Spark Plugs

Becoming Our Mothers With Better Hair

A Clean House Is The Sign Of A Wasted
Life Or A Least A Broken Computer

Women Of A Certain Age Become
Their Own "Weather Channels"

Many Thanks

Introduction

Once we women reach a certain age, we realize we shouldn't keep anything penned in – our wisdom, our emotions, our dreams, or our stomachs! Our midsections are symbolic of the many trials and triumphs we've experienced and the subsequent lessons gained from them. Over the years, they've been stuffed into an array of fashions from bellbottoms to mini skirts to maxi dresses to culottes to leggings to Capri pants. They've stomached demanding bosses, judgmental mothers–in-law, unreasonable landlords, sassy teenagers and the lame Darrin switch on "Bewitched" in 1969. They've quaked with laughter during times spent with cherished girlfriends and they've housed precious babies.

Living with ungirdled passion means you have the guts to be yourself, to let it all hang out and to enjoy the second and third acts of life, despite some of the less desirable "gifts" that come with age. So what if our waistlines are no longer as trim as they once were? We're living large in all the ways that count! The priority now is to follow our bliss, despite those wine and Entenmann's delivery trucks being really hard to keep up with!

We've also grown comfortable in our own skin – even if that skin is now spotted, loose and veiny! Those living with ungirdled passion have shed the girdles that constrained too many of our mothers – not just the nylon and spandex variety, but the societal ones as well. Our experience and insights are the foundations that serve us best. The ungirdled woman doesn't run from the changes that come with age (mostly because she can no longer run), but she accepts them with grace, dignity and good spirits - namely tequila, vodka and gin!

The purpose of this book is to highlight and celebrate the important insights that can only be gained from living and loving for the past five or six decades while laughing at the less-appreciated gifts that come with the A.G.E. syndrome. It's also to let you know you're not alone. You may be hairier, heavier, and grumpier. But you're not alone. The good news is you're also likely to be a lot wiser, happier, and more serene than you were in your 20s, 30s and early 40s.

Ungirdled women are very lucky, as growing older is a privilege that has been denied too many sweet souls we've known. So, if the privilege of growing older comes with a few annoying "gifts," we'll take it! Besides, the "gifts" that haven't killed us have only served to make ~~our drinks~~ us stronger. Yes, age truly is a gift – a gag gift. And gag gifts are intended to amuse us! Ungirdled women don't live in the past, wishing we were younger or thinner. We live in the moment and take the time to stop and Instagram the roses. So, let's take a look at those roses, thorns and all! We'll begin with that big elephant in the womb (or there about)...

Menopause And Perimenopause, Aka "Werewolf" and "Jabba The Hutt" Syndromes

We can't discuss aging without talking about menopause, also known as "the change." And a "change" it is indeed – a change akin to the transformation made by werewolves during the full moon. At times, we really do become hairy, howling monsters! At least that's what my husband might say - if not afraid to.

We can blame it all on that greedy damn Eve back in the Garden of Eden. She just *had* to have that apple (or was it quince?) Anyhoo... it wasn't like she found an éclair tree or a martini tree she couldn't resist. It was an *APPLE* tree. (Or a quince.) Thanks a bunch, Eve. Now we have menstrual cycles and periods. And pain at childbirth. And once the periods come to an end? Our ovaries start closing up shop, signaling the start of perimenopause and then comes menopause (otherwise known as female werewolf and Jabba the Hutt syndromes).

Apples are not that delicious. And, while I've never eaten a quince, I know it cannot be worth all that! I looked up the Weight Watchers points for it, and it's only one point. An éclair? Nine sinfully worth-it points. Enough said.

Once I entered perimenopause, I wanted to learn more about "the change." I turned to the medical advisor I trust most: the worldwide web.

I was confused by the difference between "peri" and regular ol' menopause. The Mayo Clinic's website defines perimenopause, also called the "menopausal transition," as "the interval in which a woman's body makes a natural shift from more-or-less regular cycles of ovulation and menstruation toward permanent infertility, or menopause." It states that women can start perimenopause at different ages, noticing the signs in their 40s or even in their 30s. As for "menopause," the Mayo clinic's site states, "Once you've gone through 12 consecutive months without a menstrual period, you've officially reached menopause, and the perimenopause period is over." I read via many different sources that perimenopause can last FOR YEARS!

One article I stumbled upon listed 35 SYMPTOMS OF MENOPAUSE! And I could check off 26! See how many you can check off. Following is that list:

1. Hot flashes, flushes, night sweats and/or cold flashes, clammy feeling (More on this in the next chapter.)

2. Irregular heart beat

3. Irritability

4. Mood swings, sudden tears

5. Trouble sleeping through the night, with or without night sweats (More on this later.)

6. Irregular periods; shorter, lighter periods; heavier periods, flooding; phantom periods, shorter cycles, longer cycles

7. Loss of libido (We'll talk more on this symptom later, which Suzanne Somers has appropriately termed "Men on pause.")

8. Dry vagina

9. Crashing fatigue

10. Anxiety, feeling ill at ease

11. Feelings of dread, apprehension, doom

12. Difficulty concentrating, disorientation, mental confusion (I'm thinking there may be more on this ... Oh! I forgot to defrost the salmon...Wait, what day is it? ... later.)

13. Disturbing memory lapses (More on this later, if I remember correctly.)

14. Incontinence, especially upon sneezing, laughing; urge incontinence (More on this later.)

15. Itchy, crawly skin

16. Aching, sore joints, muscles and tendons

17. Increased tension in muscles

18. Breast tenderness

19. Headache change: increase or decrease

20. Gastrointestinal distress, indigestion, flatulence, gas pain, nausea

21. Sudden bouts of bloat

22. Depression

23. Exacerbation of existing conditions

24. Increase in allergies

25. Weight gain (Loads more on this later.)

26. Hair loss or thinning, head, pubic, or whole body; increase in facial hair (More on this later.)

27. Dizziness, light-headedness, episodes of loss of balance

28. Changes in body odor

29. Electric shock sensation under the skin and in the head

30. Tingling in the extremities

31. Gum problems, increased bleeding

32. Burning tongue, burning roof of mouth, bad taste in mouth, change in breath odor

33. Osteoporosis

34. Changes in fingernails: softer, crack or break easier

35. Tinnitus: ringing in ears, bells, 'whooshing,' buzzing etc.

As if these 35 symptoms aren't enough, I've added few others my friends and I have experienced at this special time in life:

36. You find yourself dialing every phone number you see on bumper stickers that read, "How's my driving? Call 1-800-whatever" to report just how REALLY STUPID the driving is.

37. Everyone around you has a *really* bad attitude problem

38. You find Brad Pitt's appeal has nothing on that of carbohydrates and cannot stop eating Stacy's Simply Naked Pita Chips

39. You have an intense desire to taser those ~~stupid hippie wenches~~ trying to be helpful who say to "simply think of hot flashes as power surges." I suppose that means we are to think of the weight gain involved with menopause as "an accumulation of assets," or in my case, just plain ASS.

40. Front "bush" loses "foliage" while the "back porch" gains "vegetation!" (More on this hairy situation later.)

41. Neck and chin merge into one area, convincing you that

Return of the Jedi character Jabba The Hutt was NOT a robotic film studio creation but an actual woman in deep perimenopause. (More on this later.)

42. Special storage shed is now required to house your *facial* landscaping tools. (More on this later.)

43. Hair on your head becomes the texture of a straw broom. (The good news, though, is the hair growing out of your nose, over your lip and from your chin is baby soft!)

44. New, sudden interest in small firearms (Just a fleeting thought, however, as we know having guns around is serious, dangerous business. Tasers on the other hand...)

45. You find the quickest way to a smaller waistline is to lift up your breasts. (More on this later.)

Hopefully, it helps knowing that becoming a big, hot, mad, hairy mess is typical, and you're not alone. I say make a fun game of it! Make lemon martinis out of lemons by buying lottery tickets with the numbers that correspond with your particular symptoms and see what happens! Granted, if you're like me, you may need to buy several lottery tickets to make use of all the numbers corresponding to all your symptoms, but then you increase your odds of winning! Think of all the tasers you could buy...

My Ovaries Are Going Out of Business, and All My Clothing Is Half Off!

Many women would name hot flashes as the worst symptom of menopause. They are typically worse at night and become so severe, many women are forced to search for adult size flame-retardant pajamas. With all this sweating, do we lose any weight during menopause? NO! Just the opposite! So now there's more to undress once a hot flash strikes.

The sunshiny, ~~high~~, earth mother types will tell you that menopause is a wonderful time of transition. These are the people who tell you to think of hot flashes as power surges. Following their logic, I suppose we should tell those with STDs to think of the diseases as evidence someone once found them attractive. People who make light of hot flashes have obviously never actually experienced one, or they are sniffing, smoking or ingesting something they need to share with those of us who do. Right now!

Studies say 80% of women will suffer hot flashes at some time during perimenopause. Considering this, I have to believe the theory that global warming exists because over *40 million female baby boomers are having hot flashes at the same time* has to be accurate.

I've tried the over-the-counter remedies like black cohosh and soy. I've tried progesterone cream. I've stuck pins in a voodoo doll of Eve for eating that apple (or quince). I read about potential risks associated with estrogen replacement so I haven't tried that. (You should talk to your doctor about your personal situation, as I am not a doctor, even though I do have terrible handwriting and like to take Wednesdays off.) I've read about a couple of drugs used to treat hot flashes and the list of side effects reads like a who's who in torture. I do what's suggested: I exercise regularly, try to eat right and get enough sleep. I don't smoke. I don't drink a lot. (On Tuesdays.) Yet, no relief. I am not comforted by the fact that my mother and other women I have talked to say they still experience hot flashes in their 70s.

For me, the only bright spot about having hot flashes is that as they intensified, my periods became MIA. And while I don't miss having a period, if given the choice, I almost think I'd choose periods over hot flashes. Being anti-waste, I have put my stockpile of maxi pads and tampons to good use as perspiration catchers in my bra, armpits and other places. Now I can still frolic on the beach, skydive and go horseback riding like the feminine-hygiene-product commercials promise!

I have to think if men suffered hot flashes, we'd have a cure as fast as you can spell V-I-A-G-R-A. The only real benefit of hot flashes? I no longer need to worry about getting pregnant, because any eggs I could possibly have left have gotta be totally fried.

When It Comes To Aging, It's Best to Keep Your Chin Up. WAY Up.

When the skin around my knees lost its grip, and the veins in my legs decided to come out, I realized I should no longer wear shorts in public. When new hair growth occurred in places hair should really not appear, I stocked my vanity with just as many "landscaping" tools as my garden shed holds. Gray hairs now dye at the hands of my hairdresser every five weeks. Longer tops and jackets cover an ever-expanding silhouette. But what do you do about the wattle that seems to emerge at "a certain age?"

I started developing my wattle shortly after Nora Ephron came out with her best-selling book "I Feel Bad About My Neck" in 2006. I so admired and adored Nora, may she rest in peace. She was truly one of the funniest writers and playwrights on the planet, not to mention an incredibly talented director and producer. The world became a little duller when she left us in 2012. But, while reading that book, I did feel a little sorry for Nora regarding her neck problem. I did not yet know I should be saving my pity for my own rapidly deteriorating "neck situation."

Nora wrote that her dermatologist told her a woman's neck starts to go at age 43. That is *exactly* when it started for me. If you're reading this, and you are not yet 43, run and look at your neck in the mirror and admire it. Take photos of it. Appreciate and cherish it, because it WILL change. I don't know why Mother Nature allows this to happen. I can see no good from it, but trust me, it happens. Many a girlfriend has told me of sinking into total depression over accidentally pushing the wrong button on their iPhones and then seeing the image of themselves looking down at it just a few inches away. This is the only reason why I do not yet have an iPhone. There really needs to be a wattle-reduction app.

I like to have a reason, a rationale, for why things occur in life. So, as I often do, I turned to trusty life coach Google for an answer. I learned, via Wiki Answers, the purpose of the wattle is *"...cooling the bird, turkeys and chickens. The areas have blood flowing close to the surface and get more air flow over the blood thus cooling it somewhat as birds do not sweat."*

I am thinking Mother Nature has designed it so our wattles start to come in just before hot flashes begin so that we will feel cooler when they occur. But, Mother Nature, there's obviously a design flaw, and I'd like to register a complaint. Because despite having an impressive, citation size wattle, this chick still gets hot flashes and sweats! Additionally, if you wouldn't give us hot flashes at this stage of the game, we could at least dress in turtlenecks and scarves to cover the emerging problem!

I thought I had an ingenious strategy. Why not apply dark, self-tanning cream on the wattle to make it kind of "fade to black?" I brought this up at book club where several other friends feel they too are afflicted with wattle neck. We talked it over and decided it would just make the folds and wrinkles become more prominent and cause our faces to look as though they were floating, unattached, over our bodies.

Short of surgery, I needed a solution. While I have yet to find a permanent fix, I have come across a couple of strategies that can help "whittle the wattle," so to speak, at least for photographs.

While at the wedding of a good friend, I couldn't help but notice how great her mother looked. When I told her she hadn't aged a bit, she exclaimed, "Oh yes I have. My neck is terrible. Lemme show you what I have to do for pictures." She then called her husband over, telling him she wanted to show me how they pose for pictures. Her husband snuck his arm up behind his wife's back, reached his hand under the hair behind her neck and yanked her neck skin back. "Takes 15 years off!" he cheerfully said. That evening, I witnessed the parents of the bride employing this strategy over and over again for photos, and if they had not told me their secret, I wouldn't have been the wiser. What a beautiful relationship they have.

When I got home, I tried pulling my own wattle back from behind in the mirror, and the difference was amazing! I now have my husband do this for me when we pose for photos. I just wish I could get a hair clip to stay there and hold it back 24/7. I shared this strategy with my girlfriends, and now when the girls get together, everyone wants to have it done when posing for a photo. The problem is, we often have just seconds to prepare for the shutter click in this age of constant photo-snapping for Facebook. So, right as a photographer says, let me take a picture of you all, you hear women desperately screaming through clenched smiles, "HOLD MY NECK! HOLD MY NECK!" Sadly, some are naturally left out in the flurry of neck grabbing. I recommend designating a neck-holding photo partner as soon as you arrive at a party so you'll be ready and covered.

If you are in a new group, and without your husband, and do not feel comfortable asking a stranger to hold your neck during a photo, you can either stretch your chin way out (think Thurston Howell, III) or cutely cock your head and rest your chin on your fist so that your fist and forearm covers the offending area. Folks may wonder why the cute woman in the photo needs to hold her head up with her fist, but at least they won't be thinking, "look at the wattle on that one." NEVER, and I mean NEVER, allow your profile to be photographed once your wattle starts to come in. I want to save you from the heartache I have experienced after viewing such photos of myself. Chances are, you will never achieve a wattle as impressive as mine, though.

Of course, the neck grab and Thurston Howell and "Thinker" poses are merely band-aid solutions. I wanted a long-term fix and I was desperate enough to pay for it. As much as it would take. Up to $20. So I invested in a gadget you've no doubt seen advertised on TV. It is promoted as "the world's first progressive resistance toner for the neck, chin and jaw muscles." It's a little spring-loaded gizmo you sit on your breastbone and under your chin and do wattle crunches with. Kind of like a little pogo stick for your chin.

Logically, it didn't really make sense that using such a gadget would get rid of my wattle, but when you've got what looks like a sack of marbles hanging from your neck, you'll try anything. I read a lot of favorable reviews online PLUS, the developer had an Australian accent. Accents really add a lot of credibility for me, so I was hooked.

I only used the wattle cruncher for a few days, as it made my neck feel really sore and I personally got a headache after using it. The ads and reviews say you need to give it 3-4 weeks before you see results. I didn't feel like I could go that distance with the way my neck and head felt after using it. You might have different results. It looks like my wattle cruncher will end up unused like my treadmill. At least my unused treadmill was good for hanging clothes on. I guess I could always "bejewel" my unused wattle cruncher and wear it as an accessory to hide my wattle when positioned in place. It could catch on.

Of course, I realize there are worse things in life than developing a wattle. I know the best beauty secret is to just be happy, confident, and smile. And to keep your chin up. WAY up!

When Your Uterus Has Fallen and It Can't Get Up

"Your aunt's uterus is falling out."

This was said by my mother, matter-of-factly, regarding the *second* of my aunts to suffer uterus-falling-out syndrome. Despite her tone, my mom was, understandably, very concerned for our relative. (Before you think I am "calling out" any of my aunts, I should tell you my mom is one of eleven siblings in her family, and my father has three sisters, so it would be hard to know who I'm speaking of.)

Before my aunts came down (perhaps a poor choice of words) with uterus-falling-out syndrome, I'd never heard of it. I hadn't known it was possible for an organ to suddenly "out" itself. I found it rather unsettling.

I wanted to learn more. The most crucial question being, "Is this a *hereditary* condition?" Because my aunts are southern ladies raised to believe showing your knees is risqué, I didn't feel comfortable quizzing them about their private parts no longer being so private.

So, once again, I turned to the medical expert I trust most: Google. (Naturally, should your own uterus make a public appearance, I recommend consulting your doctor.)

I Googled "uterus falling out," and there were lots of resources. I learned uterus-falling-out syndrome is also known as uterine prolapse. One of the risk factors listed was age. But of course.

I've long known gravity is not the friend of the middle-aged woman. Our necks droop, our breasts fall, butts flatten, the skin around our elbows and knees has more folds than elaborate origami, and don't get me started on the stomach region. It seems everything starts falling and slipping. But the uterus has to get in on this act too?

According to one site I visited, up to fifty percent of women who have delivered babies vaginally will suffer from some degree of uterine prolapse! It went on to state that in moderate cases, the cervix protrudes past the vaginal opening. In the case of severe prolapse, "the entire uterus protrudes past the vaginal opening." In other words, the sun will now shine where the sun never used to shine. This brings up another question: what SPF do you apply to your uterus while at the beach if this should happen to you?

I've long looked at young women on the beach and envied their flat stomachs, lack of neck wattle, and smooth knee and elbow regions. Now I guess I'll have to add lack of uterus hanging out to the list. I can hear it now. My friends and I will be admiring a younger woman on the beach and note, "Why, that woman can't be older than 60 – her uterus has yet to show." I know they make swimsuits to minimize your waistline and your bust line. Will there be suits designed to minimize your uterine hang?

One website listed the following symptoms of uterine prolapse:

- Feeling like you are sitting on a small ball

- Difficult or painful sexual intercourse

- Frequent urination or a sudden urge to empty the bladder

- Low backache

- Uterus and cervix that stick out through the vaginal opening

- Repeated bladder infections

- Feeling of heaviness or pulling in the pelvis

- Vaginal bleeding

- Increased vaginal discharge

The site noted that many of these symptoms would become worse when standing or sitting for long periods of time. THEN, it had the nerve to state "treatment is not necessary unless the symptoms bother you," as if you have to be one picky wench not to enjoy backache, repeated bladder infections, bleeding, frequent urination, painful intercourse and A UTERUS AND CERVIX THAT STICK OUT THROUGH YOUR VAGINAL OPENING!

Of course, one treatment listed was surgery. For mild to moderate cases, a support gadget called a pessary can be worn inside the vagina to hold the prolapse in place, sort of like a brace. Today's pessaries are often made of silicone. I read that in biblical times, women would use potatoes as pessaries. There is even a popular urban legend about a woman entering an emergency room complaining that she had a vine growing from her "vaginny," with the vine actually growing from a potato she had placed there some time before. (The woman obviously didn't have fertility issues.) One would hope that if you stuck a potato in that area, you did so after careful, thoughtful deliberation. If then you notice a vine growing from that area, and it does not occur to you that it might be *due to the potato* you stuck there, I think you've got bigger fish to fry (or potatoes?) than your uterus falling out! Wouldn't you just give the vine a good yank and have the problem solved? At any rate, I think the folks in Idaho are missing out on a really good marketing campaign.

Of course, the potatoes can have the drawback of potentially causing vines to grow from that region. It's bad enough we have to resort to razors and wax to groom that area. We don't want to add pruning shears to the toolkit. Since feminine hygiene product manufacturers make something for just about everything that comes up (or in this case down) "down there," perhaps they can develop an over-the-counter treatment for uterus-falling-out syndrome. Those folks seem big on adding wings to their products. In this case, may I suggest a tampon with a parachute? Or perhaps some type of mini hot air balloon?

Victoria's Secret could get in on the act and develop special underwear for those afflicted, because you know thong underwear and string bikinis have to be glamour don'ts for the sufferers of this condition. I would think this is the one time you do want to keep something "girdled."

If this is the first you've heard of this condition afflicting older women, I'm sorry to be the bearer of bad news. Or perhaps I should say, "You're welcome." Because, if you're like me, getting older has already provided enough surprises, and being forewarned is forearmed. Now, God forbid, your uterus decides to have its own coming out party, you'll know you're not alone – and to fetch yourself a tater. I think I'm going to complain less about the skin hanging under my chin. And hope my uterus doesn't look at it and get any ideas.

Becoming A Soil Sister

I'm not sure why it is, as we grow older, we also grow to dig the beauty and pleasure of gardening. Maybe it's because, while we love our children, it's nice to raise something that doesn't sass or leave dirty dishes lying around. Or maybe it's because with declining libidos, we've reached the point where we're more interested in a man who can perform well in our *flower*beds! (I have to confess, I've been known to have peony envy! You should see my neighbor's bushes! Especially before I clip all the blooms in the middle of the night.) Whatever the reason, many of us become obsessed with gardening as we grow older.

Nothing excites us soil sisters as much as a tour of area garden centers in early spring. We love discovering a new plant variety and sharing tried-and-true favorites. Plants my neighbors and I have discovered to be especially prolific and good for sharing are: daisies, canna lilies, day lilies, irises, chameleon plant, periwinkle, and creeping Jenny. If you've never tried creeping Jenny, add a little to the edge of your next plant composition. Its chartreuse color really makes reds and purples pop, and you'll love the way it drapes over a planter's edge.

As die-hard "potheads," we live by the no-fail pot composition law of many an ungirdled gardener: "thriller/filler/spiller." If you're unfamiliar with this concept, it simply means you select something tall with a great "wow factor" as the thriller for the center or back of your planter; then something shorter and full to fill in around and just below the thriller (the filler); then something draping over the edge (like the creeping Jenny) as the spiller. We potheads are so addicted to our habit; we're constantly searching out dealers who have the "good stuff" at great prices. What will bring us down off a gardening high quicker than anything, though, are weeds! Total buzz-kills.

Yes, weeds are the gray hairs of the garden. They must be plucked or they must *dye*! These days, I use a homemade weed killer that I think might actually work *better* than all the chemical products I've purchased in the past. Plus, it saves me a lot of money and is much friendlier to the environment! I've seen slight variations of this recipe, but this is the one I have used for several years, and it has been effective in killing crabgrass, poison ivy and lots more.

- 1-gallon vinegar (I use the cheapest white vinegar I can find)

- 1 cup of salt (I never measure this – always eyeball it, and if anything, I use a little more than a cup.)

- 1 Tbsp. dishwashing liquid (I think this helps it adhere to the plant)

I mix this up in my weed-sprayer, pop in my ear buds to listen to my favorite tunes, and begin annihilating. Try it; I think you'll like it. It's beautification without environmental devastation. After all, we ungirdled women may be into doing pots, but we're not into weed!

Middle Age Has Turned Me Into A Real Mother Plucker

(Just a warning: you may find the following chapter, like getting older, disgusting, so you'll want to put on your ungirdled panties before reading further.)

As mentioned, as I've gotten older, I've developed a love of gardening and landscaping. This love of landscaping, however, does not include the pruning I must now do to my face and other parts of my body. Lately, I actually have to drag out as many tools to prune and trim up myself as I do my yard. I hear the same story from so many girlfriends. We suddenly have wild eyebrows, CHIN hairs, MUSTACHE hair, gray hairs, hairs coming out of our noses and even other places hair REALLY SHOULD NOT BE! There's so much hair, that I have often wondered if the elusive Sasquatch we've all seen the blurry photo of is actually an escaped, hacked-off menopausal woman just wanting a little privacy due to all the unwanted hair growth. Really, Mother Nature, why must we become Chia Pets?

While talking with friends about this hairy situation, one alerted me to the fact that many middle-aged women begin to get hair *in the area plumbers most like to show off while working under your sink*. I couldn't believe it, but another friend then verified she, too, had suddenly found "grass" sprouting in her "backyard!" The first friend had discovered this gift from Mother Nature's while washing in the shower. She was shocked and confused, as no one had warned her that "grass" might suddenly grow in her "backyard." She was seriously afraid her new green tea shampoo had been acting as a sort of fertilizer in that area until she heard about it happening to other women her age. I am alerting you to this possibility in case the same should happen to you to spare you the same shock. Unfortunately, I can't do anything for you when it comes to the actual grass sprouting there.

After discussing middle-aged women "sprouting grass in their backyards," my friends and I discussed the fact that the "front lawn" seems to get more and more sparse, so to speak, as we age. We wondered why that was. Shortly thereafter, I got my answer during a special episode of "Oprah" which featured a panel of gynecologists answering questions audience members were afraid to ask their own gynies. (Why the women were afraid to ask their own doctors one-on-one, but not afraid to ask strangers on nationwide TV was a bit puzzling, but I was happy to get the information, nonetheless.)

While no one asked why the backyard suddenly started sprouting grass (I guess these women had a *little* modesty and reserve), one woman DID ask the panel why vegetation in the front yard thins out as we age. One of the experts said Mother

Nature has us grow thick front lawns in our youth so that we'll trap pheromones there to attract the opposite sex for mating purposes.

This was interesting to me, because I like to know WHY things occur, the purpose of Mother Nature's designs. For instance, I know we have eyebrows above our eyes to keep sweat from dripping in them, and we have hair in our noses to keep dirt and dust from entering our lungs. Oprah's expert went on to explain that our front yards thin as we age, because *we no longer need to trap pheromones there.* In other words, Mother Nature feels since our eggs are well past their expiration dates, we are TOO OLD TO BE WORTHY OF ANYONE PAYING ATTENTION TO THAT AREA! So, I guess that also answered my question about why many of us suddenly grow MUSTACHES and a crop of "backyard" hair. Mother Nature obviously wants to *MAKE DARN SURE* we'll be too unattractive (and smelly?) for anyone to have *any* desire to "mate" with us!!

Well, Mother Nature, I've got news for you, it's going to take A LOT more than hair there, there, and even *THERE* to put off most men and husbands I know. So, while you're in charge of the hard drive, so to speak, God must be in charge of software or sex drive, and trumps you! So there!

(Dear Lord, you should know this mother plucker will probably meet you at the Pearly Gates with tweezers,

depilatory cream and personal hair trimmer in tow thanks to that mean, mean wench!)

The Number One Reason We Need More Female Architects: Going Number One!

It's not enough that our uteruses (uteri?) might decide to fall out at any minute once we get older, but our bladders seem to shrink, necessitating frequent trips to the ladies room. We go from "partying all night" to "pottying all night!" I actually think if I were magically granted the power to be in two places at once, I'd use that power to stay in bed asleep while I also frequently get up to pee.

It's not like we can stop drinking. With our dry skin, brittle nails and straw-like hair, we must stay hydrated. And if you're like me, with all the other symptoms that come with middle age, I like to stay hydrated with chardonnay, vodka and gin!

When out with girlfriends, I am always reminded of how much longer it takes women to go "number one" in a public venue than it does men. (Of course when it comes to going "number 2" at home, men have us beat by HOURS. That is another chapter. Actually another book.) Much has been written about the disparity in needed vs. actual, available bathrooms for women in public venues. (There was actually a bill before Congress regarding this issue, but it has since been flushed.) When it comes to building design, addressing the needs of women going number one really needs to be priority number one!

This disparity was never more apparent for me than while attending a local production of West Side Story in our town's hip, new, multi-million dollar theatre.

The war between the Sharks and the Jets had nothing on the one among the "ladies" in attendance when it came to using the "restroom" during intermission. Within minutes after being regaled with the theatre company's performance of "I feel pretty," I was feeling anything but as I stood in the long line that stretched from inside the ladies' room to the middle of the lobby uncomfortably waiting for my turn to "relieve" my frustration. We "ladies" watched the uptown gentlemen cruise in and out of the men's room quicker than a Kardashian can sniff out a camera. Nerves became raw, as we grew more uncomfortable and impatient, wondering if we'd be able to complete our mission before intermission was over. I really thought I was about to witness a rumble when one woman jumped the line. Once you were in and scored a stall, you knew you had to work with racehorse speed to get in, get out, wash, apply lipstick and move on.

As I escaped the war zone referred to as the ladies' room, I saw several of my "gang members" still waiting in the line that snaked through the poorly-designed facility's sparkling new lobby. I couldn't resist going up to them and singing, "Tonight,

tonight, hope you get to pee tonight..." (Actually, I could have just as appropriately sung, "There's **no** place for us...") They were only so amused.

As we grow older, not only do we experience frequent urination, but we encounter "surprise urination" too. Once we only needed a Kleenex for our noses when we sneezed or coughed. Now something called a "Poise pad" (urination pad) is required, too! Tampon advertisements promise their products will allow you to continue go swimming and horseback riding if you buy them. Poise pad advertisements should tell you you'll need their products if you ever want to jump, sneeze, cough or laugh in public again!

After consulting with trusty Dr. Google, it seems menopausal women experience "surprise urination" because our pelvic muscles weaken with age. So, when the slightest pressure is put on the bladder (from lifting, jumping, laughing or sneezing) we wet ourselves. Our bladders actually become flabby and weak. Weak bladder muscles aren't the only culprits. I read that with the decline of estrogen in the menopausal woman comes the loss of elasticity in all skin - not just the skin on our hands and faces, but that of our vaginas and urethras, too. This adds to the incontinence problem as does weight gain and previous pregnancies. Check, check and check.

Why, Mother Nature, must you make it so we older women frequently wet ourselves? Does it go back to the "we're too old to mate with" deal again? In order to ensure there is no chance any man will want to fertilize what ancient eggs we have left, you cause us to leak urine? Nice. I think the decrease in libido, increase in weight, and hairy faces and "backyards" are deterrent enough!

The makers of Poise pads refer to involuntarily peeing whenever you jump, sneeze, cough or laugh as "LBL," or "light bladder leakage." The company's website states, "A little bladder leak at the wrong time can really put a damper on your day." I am compelled to ask what is the "right" time of day? They then ask, "So why let it happen?" Like I want to "let" my bladder leak. They explain how their products help suffers of LBL by allowing you to discreetly wet your pants. That really is poise.

But, hey, pee happens. So I'll meet you in the urination pads aisle, right after a trip to the face-scaping aisle. Oh, and the produce aisle. With all that seems to be suddenly letting loose "down there," I feel like I should have a potato on hand, just in case.

I've Fought The Lard, And The Lard's Won: Fallen Soldiers in Battle Against the Bulge

Another unfortunate change that occurs with middle age is that our metabolisms slow to the speed of a teenager writing an essay that's "not due for a whole other week." We can boost the exercise, cut back on calories, and still gain weight. We actually *gain more on less fuel*. Automobile manufacturers should really study the metabolism of the typical middle-aged woman when designing their hybrid cars. Perhaps if they employ fuel injection systems with decreasing amounts of estrogen, their cars will get even better mileage.

We also seem to gain the power of regeneration, as we become like lizards: we exercise our tails off, only to see them grow back!

I have employed many "soldiers" in my battle of middle age bulge, only to see many fall. Some of these soldiers spent little time on the front line (and my behind) while others fought valiantly to no avail. If I had the strength and willpower to stick it out for a full tour of duty with any of them, I could maybe win the war. Here's a nostalgic look back at a few of those who have served me, and maybe you, as well:

Rowing machine: The rowing machine was as big as the hair of Joan Collins and Linda Evans in the '80s. Many of us learned why rowing is touted as one of the best overall exercises. We hurt all over, and in the end, hung clothes all over these soldiers.

Thigh Master: Oh, you were a convincing temptress Suzanne Somers. You seduced me into believing that if I squeezed my brownie-filled thighs together with a ridiculous smile on my face, I would look as svelte as you. But, alas, for me three proved not to be company but a crowd, and Betty Crocker won my heart – and thighs – in the end.

"Buns of Steel" Exercise Tape: For me, hard as boot camp. And the name? I can't help but think of buns – cinnamon, hot dog, hamburger, and well, in the end, they won that battle.

Cindy Crawford's Shape Your Body Workout Tape: Remember this one? It was created by "Radu," a trainer Cindy shared with Regis Philbin. I tried it, and Regis still looked better in a bikini than me. Mine was more "Body by Ragu" than "Body by Radu." Maybe you need to do it more than three times? Anyhooo…I've come to believe Cindy Crawford is not a human but a beautiful robot created by the manufacturers of make-up, skin-care and fitness products to sell their goods.

Various Pilates and Yoga Exercise DVDs: After trying several Pilates videos, I've discovered that "Pilates" stands for **P**ain **I**n **L**egs, **A**rms, **T**orso, **E**specially **S**tomach. This exercise technique is reportedly named after Joseph Pilates who is said to have developed the method of ~~torture~~ exercise while in forced internment in England at the outbreak of WWI. The folks at Guantanamo Bay should have employed it. Me? I am morally opposed to torture. Yoga poses proved equally painful and challenging to achieve. There was one yoga pose I learn to enjoy though. Maybe you like it too. Let's see...what's it called again? It's the one where you lean over the sink, breathe in and then slowly exhale as you hold a plate of brownies to your mouth. Yep! That's the one I learned to master.

Powerslide Exerciser: At best, the Powerslide Exerciser helped me perfect my Tom-Cruise-in-Risky-Business-slide into Krispy Kreme when the "hot light" was on.

Ab Rocket: Depression over my failure to takeoff on this fitness gadget launched me like a scud missile into a pint of Cherry Garcia.

A lot of these workouts guaranteed visible results in 10 days. The only visible result I ever seemed to achieve was limping around from sore muscles. I did achieve *audible* results such as whimpering during the workouts, followed by moaning and groaning when getting out of bed the next morning.

Just when I thought I couldn't feel any more inadequate in the area of fitness, I find there's one area I have totally ignored in my workouts: my vagina. One Russian woman, Tatiata Kozhevnikova, however, thinks out of the box (or I guess OF the box) when it comes to working out. In 2009, the Guinness Book of Records awarded Kozhevnikova the distinction of possessing the "World's Strongest Vagina."

This woman has balls. Literally. The then 42-year-old Kozhevnkova reported that she uses a special set of glass balls to exercise the, um, area. This is how she got her start: "After I had a child, my intimate muscles got unbelievably weak. I read books on Dao and learned that ancient women used to deal with this problem using wooden balls," she said. "I looked around, saw a Murano glass ball and inserted it in my vagina. It took me ages to get it out!" I couldn't help but think if having weak "intimate muscles" is your biggest problem, you should be counting your blessings rather than jamming an expensive GLASS ball in there.

Anyhooo...after this experience, she had some balls custom-made for her workouts. Said Kozhevnikova, "You insert one of the balls in your vagina, and it has a string attached to it with a little hook at the very end. You fix a second ball onto this hook." In this way, Kozhevnkova was able to lift 31 pounds with her not-so private area to earn the record. I understand there are videos of her working out online if you care to see them. I have not had the balls to do it.

With the timing of her win, I couldn't help but wonder if this is why Sarah Palin left her position as governor. Maybe she spied Kozhevnkova winning the title from her back porch and decided to go into training full time to take the title from the Russians! If anyone could do it, she could. You betcha! This is no lame duck, fitness-as-usual workout! At least Kozhevnikova can rest assured that due to her special workouts, she is one woman who is not likely to suffer from uterus-falling-out syndrome. At any rate, you have to agree, Kozhevnikova has come up with one un-beaver-able workout!

Despite all the fallen soldiers in my battle with the bulge, I will continue my search for the perfect workout, because what's better than being fit and healthy? Besides eating pizza and brownies? And drinking beer and wine? And lying on the couch with a bucket of kettle corn? And fried chicken, chili dogs, potato chips, hot Krispy Kremes... OK, so there are better things, but being fit and healthy *is* important.

Being an ungirdled woman, I've learned that the key thing is to be the healthiest I can be no matter what my size. All I ask is that if I'm ever murdered, someone please, PLEASE make my chalk outline about three sizes smaller. And throw some hot Krispy Kremes in the casket.

Ungirdled health tip: *Doctors and fitness experts recommend achieving a BMI or "body mass index" between 18.5 and 24.9. (BMI is a measurement tool that compares your height to your weight and gives you an indication of whether you are overweight, underweight or at a healthy weight for your height. There are lots of free, online calculators to determine your BMI number). Here's a quick way to maintain a healthier BMI: always choose shoes with a heel that's 3 inches or higher. Bam! Healthier BMI. You're welcome!*

The Skinny on What We Chubby People Know

One of the worst things to deal with when your metabolism slows is a creature known as "the naturally skinny."

My husband is one of ~~these jerks~~ the naturally skinny. A few of my favorite girlfriends also fall into this category. The naturally skinny have always been so. They have never had to diet. Their bodies seem equipped with force fields that repel fat. I, on the other hand, have never been thin. Not even in second grade. Giving birth to twins, being one in a long line of "sturdy women" in my family, and getting older hasn't helped.

I have observed that the naturally skinny sometimes forget to eat lunch. This has never happened to me. Not ever. I start thinking about lunch while having breakfast and sometimes before. It's not like my lunches are anything exciting to look forward to. They usually consist of something carefully measured out calorie-wise, like a veggie burger on a low-cal sandwich thin and one carefully counted out portion of baked chips.

I have noticed that once the naturally skinny realize they haven't eaten, they often scarf down whatever is closest – an entire bag of chips, a pack of Oreos, a couple of small farm animals – and they'll be none the fatter. Because the naturally skinny usually come packaged in a protective coating of cute, it saves me from totally hating their tiny guts for it. You also have to feel sorry for someone who forgets to eat. Still, the naturally skinny will sometimes step on a nerve, and it's not their inability to gain weight that does it.

The thing I find hard to stomach about the naturally skinny is their ~~stupid~~ well-intentioned advice on losing weight. Having the naturally skinny give advice on weight loss makes as much sense as Tiger Woods leading a fidelity seminar. I've found if you make the mistake of lamenting how hard it is to lose extra pounds in front of the naturally skinny, they will cheerfully break the "news" that "eating carbs like chips and cookies can cause you to gain weight!" and "taking in fewer calories than you burn will help you lose pounds." They submit these revelations with such enthusiasm that you want to incredulously reply, "WHAT? Wait. Seriously? Cookies and chips are *fattening*?" When my husband makes such ~~asinine~~ "helpful" remarks, I often find myself growling through Mint Milano-stained teeth, "I know *HOW* you're *supposed* to lose weight!" (And by the way, beloved friends on the Paleo Diet, I'm glad for your weight loss and everything, but you should know, if an actual caveperson from the Paleolithic era saw you turning down a Mint Milano, I have every confidence he/she would immediately begin to club you to death. Just saying.)

When Oprah had her talk show, she or one of her guests would often say of being overweight, "It's not about the food, it's about something deeper, and you're actually eating your feelings," as though you have to be suffering from some kind of deep-seated personal agony to appreciate cheeseburgers, apple fritters and Nutella. If I'm sad, yes, those things taste wonderful. But you know what? If I'm ecstatic, they are delightful. If I'm feeling indifferent, there's no difference. If I'm surprised, they taste, not surprisingly, fantastic. If I could have surgery to remove my potato-chip-appreciating taste buds, I don't think I could do it. To me, *that* would give me deep-seated personal agony! I feel chubbies need to inform the naturally skinny of something: food tastes good.

No, we chubby people are not lacking knowledge. We're lacking willpower, a good metabolism and skinny genes. We know Cherry Garcia is full of calories, but we are compassionate people who think Ben and Jerry, Sara Lee, and Famous Amos are geniuses who merit our support. We have asked the lard into our lives, and we regularly attend sundae school. We've heard you tell us over and over "nothing tastes as good as thin feels." We can't help but think you've obviously never had a hot Krispy Kreme.

What's even worse than the naturally skinny? Newly successful dieters. You've no doubt run into these people. Their loss is your pain. They will go on and on about the fat content, carb value and calories of every bite you take, plus how many minutes of roller-blading, dog sledding or water polo you'll need to do to burn it off.

Unlike newly-successful dieters, we chubbies may not treat our bodies so much as temples, but as sacred burial grounds where many a brownie and slice of pie have been laid to rest. We metabolically-challenged lovers of food are happy for our skinny brothers and sisters. Please know we want to be healthy and fit, and we would love to look like you. We actually already know the "secret" to being slim. It's the same advice we could give our skinny friends for staying on our good sides: when it comes to losing weight, it's best to keep your lips pressed together! Bless their little cholesterol-free hearts.

I will ask this, however, do these three empty pizza boxes make my butt look big?

Ungirdled diet tip: *To decrease the number of slices of pizza you eat by half, when ordering, ask the pizza shop to cut the pie into 4 slices instead of eight. I know! You're welcome! Or, you could just order salad. My recommendation for an especially delicious salad is one that comes with pizza. That's my personal favorite anyway.*

Age Has Affected My Very Sole

When it comes to aging, my feet had been the final frontier, not yet conquered. My wattle had grown in, hair started appearing where hair really should NOT appear, and my metabolism had come to a screeching halt. However, my feet had been unaffected by aging. Sadly, that too has changed.

It's sad, because I love shoes. I adore shoes. Like most ungirdled women, I believe that your heart, your wine glass and your shoe closet can never be too full.

Perhaps the biggest reason we women love shoes so much is that while our figures may change, we really don't gain weight in our feet. Nor do our feet get wrinkles. We may have fat jeans and not-so-fat jeans in our closets, but we don't have to have fat shoes. We don't look down at our feet and think, "I've gained weight," or, "I'm really looking my age." It's the one body part we can pretty much dress however we like. I like knowing that no matter what age my face or figure registers, I can always look down at my feet and be whoever and whatever I'm in the mood to be. There are no wattles, no wrinkles, and no age spots on my feet. With the right shoes, I can be a cowgirl, ballerina, athlete, rock star, and shrewd business executive – even a gladiator!

The right shoe can really transform our outfits and our attitudes. As Bette Midler has said, "Give a girl the correct footwear and she can conquer the world." If I catch my waistline in a mirror, I do not see a ballerina. But if I put on a cute pair of ballet slipper-inspired shoes, I can look down and feel like a prima ballerina all day.

Men do not understand this. One pair of sneakers, one pair of flip-flops, one pair of "black" shoes and one pair of "brown" shoes is all they think they need. They don't understand the subtle but vital differences between a black espadrille and a black peep-toe wedge, let alone the differences among and need for black tennis shoes, rain boots, sling-backs, clogs, cowboy boots, gladiator sandals, ballet flats, riding boots, suede pumps, patent leather pumps... well, YOU understand we could go on and on here. I explain a shoe-shopping spree to my bewildered husband this way: "I have multiple personalities, and they all needed new shoes!" Like many ungirdled sole sisters, when it comes to shopping for footwear, I subscribe to the "no shoe left behind" philosophy. I want to adopt and nurture every little sole. As a wise ungirdled friend says, "Remember, God never gives us more shoes than we can handle." The depth and beauty of that statement brings tears to my eyes.

Finding the right size has always been a bit challenging for me, as I wear, um, a *bit* larger size than the average woman. When

I'm asked what size I am, I like to say, "I'm a size 6, but a 10 often feels oh-so-much-more comfortable, I usually get that. But, yes, I'm a size 6."

It never fails to happen. I'm always excited as I approach the shoe section at T.J. Maxx. The size 5 shoes are always displayed first. I am giddy as I spy all the gorgeous pairs I might buy. That feeling quickly leaves after doing the walk of shame (or at my size, I guess I should say "cruise" of shame) to the size 10 aisle (dock?) to discover the size 10 shoes aren't quite as cute as their little sisters of the same style on the size 5 racks. It's like comparing puppies to old, overweight dogs. That is, if they even *have* the styles I see in the size 5 aisle in size 10. (Does that stop me from buying a pair though? You know it does not.)

Lately, age has affected my very sole, and finding the right size is not the only problem I encounter when shoe shopping. I have to make sure whatever pair I buy can accommodate my burgeoning bunions. I've also noticed the big toe on my right foot is suddenly curving sharply to the right! Why? Does this little piggy think that's the way to the market? I sure wish he'd stay home. Now I must find sandals that can detract from his wanderlust, making it harder and harder to find my "sole mates."

Then there's the "cracked heel" syndrome so many of us middle-aged women seem to suffer. Now, not only are my feet bumpy and my toes freakishly bent, my heels are as dry and peeling as the trunk of a birch tree. On more than one occasion, my husband has asked if he should fetch his belt sander to smooth them. At those times, I cheerfully suggest another place he might apply the sander.

Not only have my feet gotten wider, bumpier and drier, now they often ache. I've power-walked with a friend for years, and these days, we both notice our feet often hurt whether walking, standing, sitting or sleeping! Even expensive walking shoes are of little help. I've become way-too familiar with corn pads and callus removers. Can orthopedic shoes be far behind?

So I have two questions. First, for Father Time: why can't you leave us the ability to wear cute shoes on our feet as you make the rest of us a little less cute? It's not like I'm angling to pair a nose ring with my bifocals or a mini skirt with my varicose veins. I simply want the ability to wear some cute shoes.

And shoe manufacturers: if we can put a man on the moon, why can't we put a cute AND comfortable shoe on a woman of a certain age?

50 Is The New 30 Like Nicky Minaj Is The New Streisand

And why would we want it to be?

I am so tired of hearing "50 is the new 30!" What pressure that could be on those not-yet-ungirdled who are 50 and older, and what a load of bunk! I mean how many 30-year-old women do you know running around dressed by Chico's, reeking of Ben Gay, and shopping for corn and Poise pads? I mean, do you look at that and think "Hmmm...that looks and smells like 30 to me?"

If 50 truly were the new 30, then that would mean the following:

Hair: "Gray, coarse and straw-like is the new silky, shiny and luxurious!"

Shoes: "Orthopedic is the new stiletto!"

Stepping out: "Bunko and book clubs are the new beer pong and butt quarters!"

Indulgences: "Pedicures and Silpada jewelry are the new tattoos and body piercings!"

When a couple of longtime girlfriends and I were turning 50, one came up with the idea of getting a group of women to go to the Dominion Republic to celebrate. At first I felt so guilty doing it. After all, I had two in college to pay for, plenty of home repairs and updates that were needed, as well as the usual, monthly bills. And, once you hit fifty, you've got more than ever to pay for – colonoscopies, hair dye, wine, Poise pads, Ben Gay, wine, face-scaping tools, bail for young adult children (Just kidding! Kind of.) – the list goes on. But I am SO glad we did it. It was one of the best trips ever, and I highly recommend doing such a trip with your favorite girls. The friend who came up with the idea arranged an all-inclusive package deal at a beautiful resort, so the price was right. Granted, getting the deal meant that we were by far the oldest guests at the resort, as all the others were honeymooners in their late 20s. (There was so much newlywed groping and grinding taking place in the pools and surf we shared with the young couples, we could have all come home with a pregnancy as a souvenir if it weren't for each of us having few to no eggs left.)

It was a wonderful trip. Without husbands and children, we gabbed while lounging surfside under palm umbrellas and floating in the beautiful surf each day. We enjoyed happy hours in the pool each afternoon, then dressed for a delicious dinner we did not have to prepare each night. We even ventured into a disco one evening and turned that mother out. Yes we did! We dropped like it was lukewarm. For almost five minutes.

We called our trip the "Fifty and I Know It" tour, as LMFAO's "Sexy and I Know It" song was popular at the time. I even came up with special lyrics to the tune of "I'm Sexy and I Know It" for the occasion. You can even substitute "sixty" for "fifty" if you like. Here goes:

When I walk on by, folks be saying damn good she dye

Cuz gray roots be beat, kinda like the corn pads on my feet, yeah

This is how I roll, maybe my pants should be tummy control

Proudly have my big ass in tow

With my bladder, always got to go

Girl walkin' lil' shoddy (x3)

My back went out

Girl walkin' lil' shoddy (x3)

My back went out

When I jump or I sneeze, I release pee

Everybody stops and they starin' at me

I got Poise pads in my pants, so I ain't afraid to show it, show it, show it...

I'm fifty and I know it (x2)

Yo, when I'm at the mall, head to Chicos and that's not all

When I'm at the beach, in a skirted suit trying to hide my cheeks (whaat?)

Give me a TP roll - ladies' room – it's always time to go!

Headed to garden club, providin' service.

Cute shoes, smart shirt, folks don't deserve us.

Girl walkin' lil' shoddy (x3)

My back went out

Girl walkin' lil' shoddy (x3)

My back went out

When I jump or I sneeze (yea) I release pee (okaay)

Everybody stops and they starin' at me

I got Poise pads in my pants so I ain't afraid to show it, show it, show it, show it...

I'm fifty and I know it

Ayyy

I'm fifty and I know it

Check it out, check it out...

Jiggle, jiggle, jiggle, jiggle, jiggle, yeah (x3)

Jiggle, jiggle, jiggle, jig-yea, yea

Everything jiggles man

Can't help but jiggle, man (yea)

I'm fifty and I know it

Ayyy, yeah

But, as so often happens, I digress...

My point is, we had fun turning "the big five-oh!" We weren't ashamed of it. So, where does this thinking that we're supposed to be eternally youthful, thin and line-free come from? A lot of it seems to come from Madison Avenue - the same place that puts out magazines that have articles on how to lose 10 pounds in 30 days in the same issue that contains a story on how to make "the best chocolate cake ever!" You know - the same magazines that carry articles revealing "how to erase the wrinkles" with travel articles on the sunny Caribbean. Those magazines are giving us what they apparently think we want to hear. But is it what we want? Can we not be happy at 50 unless we think it's closer to what 30 supposedly used to be?

Sure, we 50-somethings look (and usually feel) better than our mothers did at the same age. We have a lot of time and labor saving devices our mom's didn't. We exercise. There have been many advances in healthcare and skincare. We wear sunscreen. We take supplements. We get lasik. We wait longer to have kids, and our kids wait longer to have kids. There's nothing that screams, "I'm old enough to be a grandmother" like having an actual grandchild hanging around with you. Another way we 50-somethings appear younger than our mothers did at the same age is our hair.

Remember Clairol's "Does She Or Doesn't She?" ad campaign for hair color that began in the late 1950s? You really don't have to wonder too much these days. It's reported that at least 75% of American women 25 and older color their hair in one form or another. That percentage is way up from 60 years ago. A survey taken in 1950 reported that only 7 percent of American women colored their hair. So, we're definitely less gray than our moms.

There are also differences in the hairstyles of the generations. It seems that when women in our mother's generation turned 35, there was a law that required they get a short, teased 'do that had to be carefully and painstakingly styled once a week at the salon to look as though a "Bump-It" was installed. They carefully encased this hairstyle in a special hairnet for sleeping. This hair did not get wet between salon visits – not at the pool, not at the beach, not even in the shower. Nothing ages a woman faster than a fussy hairstyle or a head of gray - or does it?

In 2009, Pamela Redmond Satran penned the book *How Not to Act Old: 185 Ways to Pass for Phat, Sick, Hot, Dope, Awesome, or at Least Not Totally Lame* to save us middle-aged women from ourselves. (Mercy! I don't think one can help from growing older in the time it takes to read that title!)

Here's an excerpt from Satran's book: *"Once upon a time we were all really cool. And in our hearts we always will be. But here's the thing: Behind our backs, the evil young changed all the rules, and now most of us are acting older than we think. So here, to help us keep our cred, is a list of style changes to consider...the point isn't to behave like a 26-year-old. It's to learn how not to act like someone a 26-year-old might snicker at."*

Satran's list contains these rules (along with many others):

• *Unstrap that Rolex (26-year-old cool types don't wear watches.)*

Just a guess: this is to aid in their habit of always being late.

• *Don't cook a roast.*

Seriously. That's in there. Apparently knowing how to deliciously serve a crowd is WAY uncool.

• *Type with your thumbs.*

Arthritis be damned! Typing and dialing on your phone with your index finger - or any fingers other than your thumbs – is so like, over.

• *Don't fear the waxer.*

That's right. Having an unkempt va-jay-jay lets everyone "including the entire locker room at the gym" know you're old, says Satran. Although we older gals have heard about the pain and the risk of disease associated with such hair removal procedures "the alternative," warns Satran, "is worse: old below the belt." I don't know about you, but I don't have a lot of folks regularly viewing this area. Even if I did, it's not like I would be passing for 30-something up until the point folks spied that particular region.

Those are just a few of the many ways Satran lists for us to pass for phat, sick, etc. in her book. I thought I'd share some tips of my own for how not to act old based on *my* personal observations of today's whippersnappers:

• *Do not wear your trousers any higher than mid-way up your butt crack.*

• *Only wear thong underwear even though, truly, it makes as much sense as using a piece of scotch tape instead of a baggie to wrap your sandwich. Make sure the top of your underwear can show above your pant line.*

• *Do not own or even rent your own place. Move back in with your 'rents.*

• *Blather incessantly on your bluetooth as you "shop" and "drive."*

• *Refer to the biological father of your offspring as your "baby daddy."*

• *Spend a large portion of your income on overpriced coffee drinks instead of brewing your own at home.*

• *Decorate your room (since you don't have a house) with pizza boxes, dirty plates, dirty laundry and Red Bull cans.*

I know Satran's book was written for fun and I found it enjoyable. Thankfully, ungirdled women don't care what 26-year-olds think of us or worry about how old, sick, phat or dope we look. We choose to happily be ourselves, hairy va-jay-jays and all, and enjoy our pot roasts while the younger generation max out their credit cards at Taco Bell. Yes, we have fuller waistlines, but we have fuller hearts, brains and bank accounts, too!

No, I wouldn't go back to being 30, because I wouldn't know all that I know and wouldn't be surrounded by such wonderful longtime girlfriends who have learned so much as well. I'm glad I'm not the same person I was at 30, and I hope to have learned, loved and laughed a lot more by the time I'm 70. Good lord, can you imagine what they will be doing with va-jay-jays then?

Which brings us to...

Bling For Your Private Thing

We women like to dress things up. We slip iPhones and iPads into decorative covers; we put bows on our mailboxes at Christmas time; and we even buy rubber gloves adorned with jewels and ruffles to cheer us while performing household chores. What isn't better with a little window dressing? I can now think of one thing. It was brought to my attention that many yet-to-be ungirdled women have gotten into "vagazzling." That is decorating their nether regions with stick-on jewels and crystals. (Vagina + bedazzle = vagazzle.) Seriously.

I understand this practice has been around for a few years, and it really took off when Jennifer Love Hewitt talked about her own bejeweled bits on the "George Lopez Show" in 2010.

I was intrigued and confused. I needed to learn more, and I had a lot of questions, such as, "What are the health risks?" "Where does one purchase va-jay-jay jewels?" "Am I spelling "vagazzle" correctly?" "Just how many times did Jennifer's mother drop her on her head as an infant?" "Can you still go swimming and horseback riding?" And the biggest question of all, "Why?"

I consulted the internet. I found demonstrational videos on YouTube. There was even a vagazzling fan page on Facebook. Here is what I learned:

There are professionals who will adhere the jewels on the "area" for you. You can check with your local spa. (And to think I felt so vulnerable and nervous as a young girl when getting my ears pierced!) You can also purchase vagazzling jewels online and do the deed yourself. You can snatch up a wide array of colors and patterns – I bet you can even get words put there. Mine would read "Closed For Business" or perhaps "Think Out of the Box."

One needs to be free of all lotion, body oil and HAIR in the area before having the adhesive-backed jewels applied. Acrylic adhesive or eyelash glue may also be used to hold the jewels or crystals in place. One can expect to hang onto their jewels for up to three days. It is recommended that you wear loose clothing to extend the life of your vagazzling. I suppose that after one went to all the trouble, they'd get more than a little crotchety if the jewels quickly fell off.

As to why it's done, vagazzlers report it gives them a feeling of empowerment and sexual allure. I would imagine they could also add a feeling of chafing and irritation to the list.

If I'm going to spend money on jewelry, it's going to be on something I can see and appreciate. Growing up, our mothers told us to always make sure we had on good underwear when we left the house in case we got in a traffic accident and medics might get a glimpse of our undergarments. Will mothers now need to remind their daughters to "put on your good va-jay-jay jewels" before leaving the house?

I have to believe the vagazzling craze will be short-lived. Can you just imagine someone reading your last will and testament and announcing, "...and to my precious granddaughter, I leave my coveted va-jay-jay jewel collection?"

The Right Mix of Thongs and Granny Panties in Our Friendship Drawers

While ungirdled women have done away with girdles, we still have a need for a variety of other undergarments: slips, panties, smoothers, hosiery, and let's not forget bras – support, enhancing, minimizing, athletic, strapless, racer back, etc.

Thinking about the variety of undergarments we all possess, I can't help but notice how different types of underwear can be a lot like the different friends in our lives. Some garments are constricting and controlling, while others are fun, but don't provide the support we need. We choose different underwear to suit various outfits, moods and occasions. Ungirdled women have learned the value of doing the same with friendships. See if you don't have the following mix of friends in your "friendship drawer:"

Spanx – Most of us benefit from wearing Spanx now and then, and we all benefit from having Spanx friends. You know the ones I'm talking about. Way better than girdle-type friends who constrict and all-but-suffocate you, Spanx friends provide the right amount of support. They help us be the best we can be. They may not be the most fun, but it sure is a relief to know they are always there in life (and the underwear drawer!) when we need them.

Athletic bras – These are friends who aren't afraid to face a challenge and are there to sweat it out with you during the most demanding times. They may not be flashy or concerned with appearances, but they can take the heat. These are the friends who are the first to show up when a loved one dies, who take you to chemo, who support you through a divorce.

Special-occasion lingerie – These are the pretty, fashionable and/or fun friends you have a ball with at parties and special events. They may be a little "too much" for everyday life, but it's blast to go out with them once in a while and escape everyday doldrums.

Granny panties – These are the comfortable, let-it-all-out friends you are grateful to have around most of the time. They are 100% all-natural cotton, no-nonsense types that have you covered. Maya Angelou says, "I've learned that people will forget what you said, people will forget what you did, but people will never forget how you made them feel." I know I like the way granny panty friends make me feel.

Thongs – We've all had these types of friends in our lives - the ones who are irresistible at first. They seem so cute, so fun, but then bite us in the butt when we least expect it. Disappointed, we realize there's not much substance there, that synthetic is not for us. When we're younger, we may not have had the self-confidence or maturity to stay away from thongs, but eventually, we figure out that if they are irritating and don't support us, then why bother? (By the way, did you know they started making SANITARY NAPKINS FOR THONG UNDERWEAR? Using this type of feminine "protection" must be like mowing your lawn with fingernail clippers, but I digress.) Maya Angelou has also advised, "The first time someone shows you who they are, believe them." That brings us to...

Castoffs – Just as you sometimes "outgrow" certain underwear, you realize certain friends are no longer a good fit. Maybe you've grown apart or maybe you've realized someone is too much of a thong or girdle for you. As with underwear, you feel guilty throwing something out. You think about how cute or fun the friend (or underwear!) is and how much you have invested. But, if it's uncomfortable and bites you in the butt, it's not working, and it's best to cut your losses. You may relegate certain underthings to a rarely opened, out-of-sight drawer. It's perfectly OK, and sometimes the healthiest thing to do with certain friends. After all, you're not wearing the same underwear you did at 6, 16, and 36!

The bottom line? (Pardon the pun!) Just like underwear is the foundation of your outfit, friendships are the foundation of your wellbeing. Countless studies have shown that friendships improve your outlook and attitude, boost your immune system, extend your life, and enhance the quality of it.

I think what many studies fail to mention is something we know innately: it's the *right combination* of friends that provides these benefits. Because, like undergarments, some are trendy; some are classics. Some hold up through hot water while others require special, delicate handling. And some will stick with you through thick and thin.

Yes, support, not bondage, is the key to undergarments for the ungirdled woman. This is true of swimsuits, too. One ungirdled friend jokes that when she lays her bathing suit on the bed (a sturdy, well-engineered one piece with cups and a tummy control panel); it looks as though she's still in it. Now that's leaving an impression!

As long as the majority of our friendships (and underwear!) are based on what's comfortable, complimentary and supportive, we'll have great foundations!

Shift Happens. It's Best To Be A Man About It.

On the road to becoming fully ungirdled, we women worry ourselves crazy over how we feel our bodies look, focusing on what we perceive to be every imperfection. As we get older, the imperfections seem to multiply. Shift happens. EVERYTHING droops. The quickest way to deduct inches from our waistlines is to lift up our breasts. Our bottoms have fallen quicker than our stocks. We haven't quite reached the winter of our lives, yet many body parts have already flown south for it! Once we reach a "certain age," we can exercise and watch what we eat, following the recommendations of the food pyramid, yet we become shaped like it!

The way many *girdled* women deal with the changes in their bodies that come with growing older is with cosmetic surgery. Ungirdled women are all for looking our best, but this cosmetic surgery thing has gotten out of hand. There are some women that have their breasts lifted so high; they can now have a mammogram and dental x-rays at the same time!

Not only are people paying an arm and a leg for new breasts or a new face, the price for "enhancements" sometimes includes a woman's good health. Women have sometimes suffered severe side effects from cosmetic procedures including, while rare, death! Talk about being a real sleeping beauty!

Growing up, our mothers warned us not to shell out 39 cents for a can of peas if it was bulging as it might contain botulism. Now they want hundreds of dollars to inject a little into your face. Botox is reported to eliminate your wrinkles AND your expressions. Ungirdled women want to share all our moods with the world.

The truth is, the more ungirdled we become, we realize that worrying over wrinkles and body image is a senseless waste of time. First, worry won't change anything. Second, it's impossible to reach the magazine cover ideal that's constantly shoved at us. As we have learned, those images are a product of makeup, lighting, airbrushing and Photoshop, certainly *not* worry or even extreme exercise and diet regimens. Third, it *really doesn't* matter. What matters is that we are healthy, happy and strong. I've known far too many wonderful people who have been denied the privilege of growing older. I bet all of them – especially those who had to leave children behind – would love to come back as any one of us, "imperfections" and all.

A good friend's husband once said to me, "What you women need to understand is, to us men, God did not create a single ugly naked woman. Only beautiful ones."

So, when it comes to body image, we ungirdled women can

really take a lesson from the guys. Think about it. Why can't we view our bodies as men view our bodies? Or as men view their own bodies? And, why can't we cut ourselves the same breaks we cut them? While we see what we perceive as imperfections in men's bodies, we forgive them. We may notice the hair on his back. And coming from his ears. And his nose. And off his head. And that weird thing happening with his toenails. And while our butts seem to spread, theirs disappear! Jeff Foxworthy jokes that an old man's butt looks like you made a frog stand up and put on a pair of double-knit pants! (Look around and see for yourself! So true!)

All this happens to most aging male physiques, and yet, nearly every man we know will proudly parade around in his birthday suit as though it's haute couture. We see that it's bargain basement, but we love and value them anyway. We deserve the same love for and from ourselves regarding our own bodies.

Our bodies have served as well. They have carried children, nursed those children, and bathed and cradled those little ones. They swim in the ocean, walk our beloved pooches, dance to our favorite songs, enable us to make loving homes, allow us to give others a helping hand and so many other wonderful things. When you think of all the ways our bodies serve us, despite the abuse they take, they are indeed beautiful!

Ungirdled anti-wrinkle tip: *The great, natural beauty Sophia Loren takes a more organic approach to combating wrinkles. She reportedly uses olive oil, lightly patted on her face, as a moisturizer each night before sleeping. My home remedy of choice is Duncan Hines Chocolate Lover's Double Fudge Brownie mix. Here's what you do: whip up a batch, adding walnuts (they have antioxidants and are really good for you in that they are delicious), cook and eat. To me, a fuller, fatter face is a safer, easier, less expensive and tastier way to diminish the appearance of wrinkles than injections and surgery. You're welcome! (By the way, if you try this – and you should - just be forewarned that the first 11 brownies will taste like delicious chocolate, but the 12th will taste more like regurgitation. I know, weird, right? Can't explain it, but wanted to warn you about it.)*

Body Parts Aren't The Only Things That Wander With Age

You've no doubt heard of the "Insanity" workout. Many an ungirdled woman practices the "memory loss workout." You know the one where you go into a room, not know what you went into it for, then go back to the first room, only to remember what you needed from the second room, so you go back to it. In a survey (of myself), I found the average woman covers about 17.3 miles a day this way. It's like our minds see that our breasts and the skin around our necks, knees and elbows have wandered off, and they decide to follow suit.

What makes focus and concentration harder to accomplish is the fact that an ungirdled woman has a lot on her plate. There's housework to avoid, Kardashians to keep up with, the race to get to Krispy Kreme while the "hot" sign is lit, and that Grey Goose is not going to drink itself. It's easy to get off task. At any given moment, many an ungirdled woman is just seven Pinterest pins away from accomplishing a minor task.

And our memories! They're shot! It's like they... well, I forget. If you're like me, your memory is so random. You can remember what you paid for a certain shrub and where you purchased it five years ago, but can't remember what you ate for dinner last night. Some of us call these lapses in memory or moments of absentmindedness a case of brain farts or the act of "geezin'." Following are some examples I am providing to assure you you're not alone when it comes to brain flatulence.

I've seen two brilliant, otherwise very "with it" women I know unintentionally walking around with two different shoes on. That is, they got dressed at home in the morning and unknowingly left the house wearing a right shoe from one pair of shoes and a left shoe from an entirely different pair of shoes and didn't realize it until they were at work. Both said they put on the different shoes to see which went better with what they were wearing, got distracted, and left the house that way. One had paired a navy pump with a gray slingback. Didn't notice it until long after she'd made a sales call to a client's place of business.

Wanda Sykes jokes about this getting flaky syndrome in her stand-up act. She said she was walking out of a store one day, talking to a girlfriend on her cell phone, while LOOKING FOR SAID PHONE in her purse. Distressed at not seeing her cell phone in her bag, she said to her friend, "I can't find my phone! I must have left it in the store!" It was only when her friend responded with, "Oh, do you want me to CALL you back?" that she realized she was talking on it. I shared this story with my gynie while getting my annual exam, and she reported she had recently done the same thing! She was frantically searching through her laundry for her cell phone as she was talking to her girlfriend ON IT.

Another girlfriend wanted to treat her husband to a special, three-day getaway for their anniversary. On the appointed departure day, they got up at o-dark thirty, put their bags in the car, dropped the dog off at her parents' house, made the trek to the airport, parked in long term parking, carried their luggage inside, waited in line to be told by the ticket-taker that their tickets were for passage the FOLLOWING day! Her mind just went on vacation a day early is all.

The upside of all this is our secrets are super safe with our girlfriends now, as they have trouble remembering whose secret is whose!

My Perfect Sleep Number Is Chardonnay.

While I'm glad to be a middle-aged woman, there are some things I envy about younger women: the smooth skin around their elbows and knees, their lack of wattle, and perhaps most of all, their ability to sleep through the night.

You'd think that because we ungirdled women seem to forget everything – including our troubles – we would get a good night's sleep. Not so. From worrying about teens who want to be out partying all night; to having weak bladders causing us to potty all night; to hot flashes that keep us repeatedly tossing off covers and later waking back up shivering from dampness and lack of covers; to snoring mates; we average about 117 minutes of sleep over eight hours of bed time each night. No wonder we're now extra dingy during the day!

I read that the majority of women between the ages of 35 and 55 won't sleep well in the four to eight year period before menopause (perimenopause), and that this group of women is more likely to experience insomnia than any other. I believe it, but I have also talked with a lot of women over 55 who still have problems sleeping through the night due to incontinence, hot flashes, snoring husbands and joint pain.

When it comes to staying asleep, we've tried it all. Exercising earlier in the day. No caffeine several hours before bed. No eating before bed. Warm baths before bed. Warm milk before bed. Warm baths in milk before bed. (I joke that chardonnay is my perfect sleep number, but lots of studies have shown that while alcohol may help you fall asleep, it has the undesired effect of keeping you from *staying* asleep.)

In desperation, many have tried a popular prescription sleep aid, and we've heard the amazing stories about what some do under the influence of the drug, like unconsciously binge eating and ordering thousands of dollars of merchandise from home shopping channels! After hearing such stories, I bet you have the same question I do: How quickly can I get some of that stuff? At least I'd have fun overnight while not actually sleeping!

While I don't have the solution for getting a good night's sleep while middle-aged, I hope it will help you rest a little easier to know that you're not alone and that insomnia at this age is, unfortunately, perfectly normal. Sweat dreams!

Sex Drive in Park; Needs Spark Plugs

It's a cruel fact of life that as we get older, our memories and our skin's elasticity aren't the only things to leave us. Our libidos seem to have run away with them while our mates continue to have "booty call" on speed dial.

My girlfriends and I have often talked of our frustration with this disparity between the sexes. When it comes to "getting busy," the men in our lives are like rabbits – Energizer bunnies to be more exact. Their batteries are "Eveready," while ours always seem to need a jumpstart. Why can't we have at least half the sex drive they do, and why can't they clean up half us often as they want to hook up?

We ungirdled women love our men, and we like getting amorous *occasionally*. It's just that we've hit the age where having sex and selecting the exact size Tupperware for leftovers are pretty equally satisfying. I've read that changes in hormonal levels are to blame. Suzanne Somers has called the loss of libido that occurs for women during middle age as "Men on pause." She's pretty much nailed how we feel about getting nailed during this period of our lives.

As I said before, at this stage of the game, we tend to be more interested in a man that can perform well in our flowerbeds.

An ungirdled woman knows that the right partner is a wonderful enhancement in her garden of life. She also knows he is not the total landscape.

Consequently, for most ungirdled women, it's not the front of a man's pants we're most interested in. We like to see a big bulge in the right back pocket where he keeps his wallet. If a man wants to impress a woman of a certain age, he shouldn't spend his money on a pill to get his unit up but his time on an investment tip that will get his net worth up. That will excite us almost more than anything he does in the bedroom. Except, perhaps, picking up his dirty socks and boxers.

And forget "Sex and the City." It was a fun television show, but so NOT real life. Real women, ungirdled women, are more into "Help and The Laundry Room." If your man will do you AND the laundry, then so much the better! Nothing gets a woman in the mood like a little help with household chores. It's been said that no man has ever been shot while doing the dishes! A woman's arousal depends on so many things – mood, if the dishes are done, if the kids are asleep, if her legs are shaved, if candles are lit... A man's arousal just depends on if you're available. Often, your attendance is not even a requirement!

My girlfriends and I agree that not only are men into greater frequency; they're into greater "variety" when it comes to intimate moments. I say when your man tells you of a sexual fantasy they want to live out that you may not be up for, you should counter with one of your fantasies. Tell him if he'll accompany you on a five hour shopping spree at the outlet mall or an evening at the ballet without complaining, then you'll reciprocate with his "ideal date." Chances are, you'll be off the hook. If not, at least things will be tit for tat, or shop for tit, or ballet for tit, or whatever the case may be.

Becoming Our Mothers With Better Hair

Despite all the ways today's older women are different than their mothers were at their age, there are some ways in which we are alike. You know you've done it and been shocked and horrified when it happens: you find yourself spewing a "momism" you *never* thought you'd repeat. Following is the story of the first time I heard one of my mother's most memorable "momisms."

I was 11 and had just overheard a couple of older girls whispering about French kissing. I ran home to ask my mom what "French kissing" was. I felt pretty certain it must be what cartoon skunk Pepe Le Pew was always doing to Penelope, the poor, striped cat he was forever chasing and mistaking for a female skunk. Remember how he would mutter "Oh Cherie," as he rapidly kissed his way from her terrified hand to her trembling shoulder? That was some fancy kissing — the likes of which I'd never otherwise seen. Pepe was French, so that *had to be* what French kissing was. I would just verify it with dear ol' mom.

"Mom, what's French kissing?" I asked as I bounded into the kitchen where she stood at the sink prepping dinner. She turned to look at me with the most shocked and horrified expression and shouted, **"IT IS UPPER PERSUASION**

FOR A LOWER INVASION, AND THAT IS ALL YOU NEED TO KNOW!"

I ran to my room feeling more confused than ever. "What is *persuasion*? What is a *lower invasion*?" I wondered. Whatever they were, they were obviously evil and wrong. I was certain of a couple of things, however. I would never again ask my mother *anything* about kissing, and Pepe Le Pew was a *really bad* skunk.

"French kissing is upper persuasion for a lower invasion" is just one of the many "momisms" that puzzled and tormented me growing up - momisms I promised myself I would never say to my own children. But, despite our best efforts, my girlfriends and I confess we are becoming our mothers – sans the short, fussy hairstyle and girdle – when it comes to spouting off popular momisms.

We don't mean to do it. We don't want to do it, but then it just happens. Our children do something, and before we can blink, we've said the dreaded momism. Think about the momisms you heard from all the moms you knew growing up. If we lived in a world true to the momisms our moms most famously quoted, we'd live in a world where:

• There is a steady decline in population resulting from people jumping off of cliffs right behind all their friends.

• Most people have at least one eye poked out.

• Nearly everyone walks around with horrid, contorted facial expressions "frozen" in place because they ignored repeatedly warnings from their mothers that their faces would indeed freeze that way.

• Health care reform includes and promotes, above all else, the wearing of "good," clean underwear, because — as we all know — doctors will absolutely refuse to perform life-saving surgery on anyone *not* wearing "good" and clean underwear. This plan includes keeping an extra clean pair of underwear with you because, let's face it, if you are involved in a catastrophic event, chances are your underwear will not remain "clean," and that's not good.

Some of the momisms that most confused and puzzled me growing up include:

• **"If you break your leg climbing that tree, don't come running to me."** As if you could. I guess you were supposed to lie there until help from a stranger came and hope that stranger wasn't bearing candy. This warning came from the same woman who would be terribly worried if you didn't call to check in, because not knowing your whereabouts meant you were most likely lying hurt in a ditch "somewhere." Lying in a ditch hurt "somewhere" was a tragedy. Breaking your leg as a result of climbing a tree she told you not to? Well, you'd better go tell your sob story to someone else, Missy!

• When handing down restriction and discipline, **"This is gonna hurt me a whole lot more than it hurts you."** Seriously? Do you really think so? Then, by all means, let's swap places. You stay in my room every day after school for two weeks, and I'll make the sacrifice of watching "Days of Our Lives" while having a bowl of chocolate ice cream.

• **"To me, you'll always be my baby."** This was confusing because it came from the same woman who would also frequently say, **"You're old enough to know better!"**

Then there were the momisms that truly frightened me:

• **"Just wait 'til your father gets home!"** Poor dad.

• **"I hope you have kids just like you when you grow up!"** Didn't this mean the one verbalizing this wish would then have grandchildren committing whatever horrible deed you were at the time? Grandchildren they begged you to hurry up and have already? And wouldn't you have to engage in the act of "a lower invasion" to do so?

• **"Stand still so I can smack you!"**

• **"I've got eyes in the back of my head, that's how I know!"** Yikes! Remember that scary, sci-fi "walnut" episode of "The Dick Van Dyke" where Laura comes out of a closet full of walnuts with eyes in the back of her head? (It was actually a dream Rob had after watching a sci-fi movie on TV) Good stuff that still holds up today.

• While fighting with a sibling and whining to mom about it, you might hear, **"Knock it off or I'll give you something to cry about."** Or the equally unsettling, **"Go outside and don't bother me again until someone is bleeding."**

• **"Shut that door! Were you born in a barn?"** You're like, "I don't think so. Weren't you there, mom? You'd remember better than me."

• And, finally, this gem I heard as a teenager when a friend and I were at her house getting dolled up for a night on the town. Her mother told us, "You girls have a good time, and **be sure not to go any place that, if the world were to come to an end tonight, the good Lord wouldn't go in there to get you."** Double yikes! The only thing that died that night was our enthusiasm and desire to get into trouble. Mission accomplished, Mom!

Of course, there were plenty of wise and meaningful momisms, too:

• **"It's nice to be important, but more important to be nice."** This is one I've caught myself saying plenty of times. Still, I'd like to try out "important" just once or twice and see how it feels.

- **"Just because you can (or can afford to) do something doesn't mean you should."** I confess this became my mantra when fighting the urge to order a taser to assist in disciplining my beloved boys while they were teens.

- **"Treat everyone you meet as though they've been a friend your entire life."** I would add, "Especially if they are in possession of a nice boat, vacation home, or prescription pad."

- **"If you can't say anything nice, don't say anything at all."** Good advice, and one momism I've said many times to my two. There are super cranky periods that all teens seem to experience, that if they were to truly follow this advice, they'd be silent for days or weeks at a time.

- **"Eat your vegetables! There are children starving in China (or insert some other foreign land here) who would love to have them!"** You're thinking, "Really? Well let's pack 'em up and ship 'em off! Kill two birds! I won't have to eat the miserable things, and we'll make someone else happy!"

Other momisms I've been guilty of letting slip include:

- **"Because I said so!"**

- **"Money doesn't grow on trees."**

- **"You'll understand once you have children of your own."**

Why do moms say these things? As one friend so eloquently said of mothers, "They are our caretakers, our joy source, our energy packs and our compasses."

Mothers take the awesome responsibility of keeping their children safe, happy, healthy and on the "straight and narrow" very seriously, and will do (or say) anything necessary to accomplish that task. As another friend said, "No matter how absurd I thought the momisms I heard were, they had a habit of coming to fruition." Isn't that the aggravating truth?

Remember asking your mother why she was being so hard on you and making your life miserable? Remember her response? It likely went something like, **"It would be a lot easier to let you do what you want to do and not do or say anything at all."** Now that I'm a mom, I know that is also so true, and I've expressed the same to my children.

Like me, you are probably as thankful as I am to have had mom's advice over the years. It made me a better, more thoughtful, cautious, and healthier person who, to this day, never leaves the house without clean underwear, is in grateful possession of both eyes, and does NOT have potatoes growing behind her ears!

A Clean House Is The Sign Of A Wasted Life Or A Least A Broken Computer

Confession time. When it comes to living with ungirdled passion, there is an area with which I really struggle: housecleaning. When it comes to doing it, like most women, I hate it. I mean I REALLY hate it. Truly. The bad thing is, like most women, I adore having a clean home. There's very little I like better. I also love to have people over, but I feel I must have my house really clean before I can do it. There lies the conflict and the inner turmoil.

When I go to someone's house, I realize the last thing I think about or pay attention to is how clean his or her home is. I am too busy laughing, connecting, and having fun. So I've long wondered why I have such angst about getting my home in "apple pie order" before company arrives. I think I've figured out the answer.

Like many an ungirdled woman, I grew up with a mother who kept a pristine home. So neat and clean, it seemed to be the number one priority. I wish I had a dollar for every time I heard growing up, "Clean up these clothes/dishes/papers right NOW! What if someone were to DROP BY and SEE THIS?" I'd have had enough to pay a housekeeper to do a weekly cleaning of my home throughout my entire adult life. Consequently, I grew up thinking that having folks "drop by" and seeing something out of order was about the absolute worst thing that might ever happen to you in life (outside of getting in a serious accident without good underwear on.)

Probably one of the reasons many of us hate housework so much is because it's a job that's never finished. What you do is constantly undone. It's like Joan Rivers says, "You make the beds, you wash the dishes and six months later you have to start all over again!" For those with kids at home, cleaning your house before they are grown and out of it is equal to shoveling snow as a blizzard starts. And, if you think about it, you really can't get anything clean without getting something else dirty. It's is a lose-lose situation with cleaning!

There are a few ~~crazy wenches~~ women who say they actually like cleaning. But they are in the minority. The late, great Erma Bombeck said, "My second favorite household chore is ironing. My first is hitting my head on the top bunk bed until I faint."

The only woman I can personally think of who gets all tingly with excitement about housecleaning is Martha Stewart. Tim Allen once joked about Martha's unfortunate incarceration saying, "Boy, I feel safer now that she's behind bars. O.J. & Kobe are walking around; Osama Bin Laden too, but they take the one woman in America willing to cook, clean and work in the yard and haul her ass to jail."

If, like me, you're still struggling with shame when it comes to having a less-than-perfectly-spotless abode, I have some tips for handling unexpected guests.

• Leave your vacuum or a duster out at all times to give guests the impression that they've caught you in the middle of the drudgery. OR,

• Keep a pair of crutches near the door so you'll be able to hobble on them as you greet unexpected guests. Now drop-ins will see you haven't been able to clean AND you're not up for company. A sling or faux cast will work equally well for this purpose.

• Get some of that yellow crime scene tape and put it around your entrance. I found some at the Five Below store. Tell drop-ins you've just been ransacked. For extra authenticity, throw in a, "I just hope they find the bastards who did this!"

Another thing I like to do to make myself feel better about my non-June Cleaverness is watch "Hoarders." Nothing will make you feel better about how you don't keep house than an episode of "Hoarders."

Sometimes I think, "What I need are the right products and some good strategies to make the job easier and myself more efficient." Consequently, I have an arsenal of infrequently-to-rarely-used cleaning solutions and gadgets. One product I was surprised to learn is an effective household cleaner is vodka. I saw Kirstie Alley on "Oprah" a few years ago talking about her early career as a housekeeper. She said she favors using the cheapest vodka she can find as a household cleaner since it is earth-friendly, has no odor and really makes your home sparkle. I couldn't help but think that by using a slightly more expensive vodka as a beverage, you could make your personality sparkle and your home seem less offensive to you without actually cleaning or sweating or anything.

I say keep your home clean enough to be healthy, but dirty enough to know you have fun. I say we messies tell any guests bothered by our the state of our homes, "Please make yourself at home! Clean my house!" After all, being ungirdled women means we are bright, creative people who can always think of better things to do than housework!

Women of a Certain Age Become Their Own "Weather Channels"

Living on the Virginia coast, I keep close tabs on the weather July thru October for the possibility (or maybe I should say "probability") of a hurricane. I fixate on The Weather Channel's Jim Cantore the way other women obsess over George Clooney. Watching the Weather Channel makes me think that, for those living with a middle-aged woman, it must be like watching that channel 24/7. Let's examine:

Each morning, we experience **dense, heavy fog** that only dissipates once the right amount of coffee is administered to **upper levels**. Even after the fog lifts, we still experience **hazy conditions** while trying to remember if we put on underwear and where we left the car keys.

At the beginning of each summer, a **tropical depression** will typically occur when we try on swimsuits. This makes conditions favorable for a **cloudburst** with **heavy precipitation** in higher regions (eyes) that is almost always followed by a **mudslide** in dessert or cocktail form to provide relief. Conversely, a **Bermuda high** is achieved when we find shorts long enough and flattering enough to wear in lieu of said swimsuit.

Fluctuations in progesterone and estrogen levels bring about severe **atmospheric disturbances** such as **flash floods** (more tears) all **hail** breaking loose, or **cold fronts** experienced by our significant others.

Sudden **heat waves** leave us covered in **dew** at the same time **"snow drifts"** suddenly appear at our hairlines. Certain regions, such as elbows and knees, experience **severe drought**.

We now find it necessary to practice **deforestation** of our faces. A **solar eclipse** occurs whenever small children stand in the shadow of our ever-widening **"full moons."** Our mountainous regions begin to shift, creating **upper level lows** (droopy breasts) requiring well-engineered **frontal systems** (bras) to keep them in place.

One good thing about being this age is that many of us find pleasure and happiness in gardening, bringing about a welcome and therapeutic **"Greenhouse effect."**

The bad news is, efforts to control the effects of aging seem to be as effective as trying to control the weather. To make things sunnier, I do recommend that mudslide in both dessert and cocktail form!

Many Thanks

I'm so glad we had this time together to commiserate and celebrate what it means to be a woman aging with ungirdled passion! I thank you from the bottom of my heart for reading "Aging With Ungirdled Passion." You are sweeter than a dozen hot Krispy Kremes! I hope you have enjoyed this book and will look for upcoming titles in the Ungirdled series. Out soon will be "Ungirdled Passion's Guide To Men: A Look At The Habits of Those Possessing The WHY? Chromosome." In the meantime, I thought I would share some alternate titles I had for this book:

What to Expect When You're Menopausing

Mad Women

Dame of Groans

Chardonnay for Elephants

The Hungry Dames

Where the Wild Hairs Are

Whole Lotta Shakin' Goin' On

Got Milk? Of Magnesia?

The Sisterhood of the Traveling Breasts

A Series of Unfortunate Symptoms

Made in the USA
Charleston, SC
26 April 2013